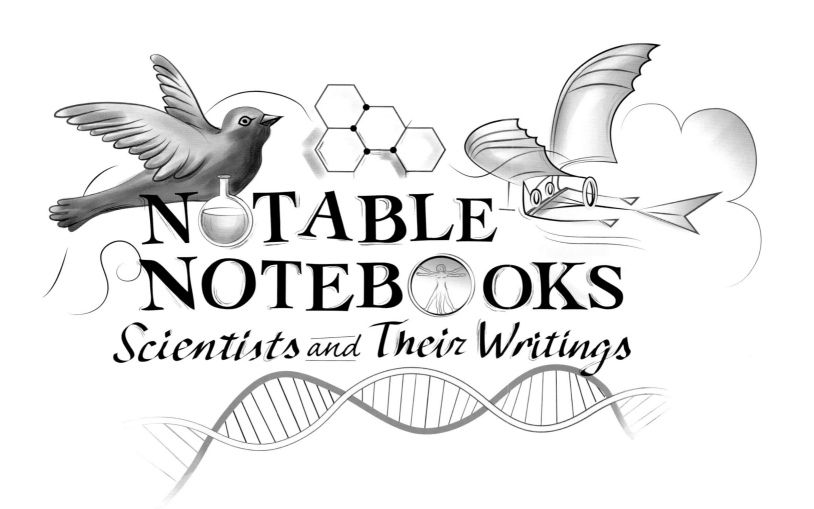

N☉TABLE NOTEB☉OKS
Scientists and Their Writings

National Science Teachers Association

Claire Reinburg, Director
Wendy Rubin, Managing Editor
Rachel Ledbetter, Associate Editor
Amanda O'Brien, Associate Editor
Donna Yudkin, Book Acquisitions Coordinator

ART AND DESIGN
Will Thomas Jr., Director
Linda Olliver, Cover, Interior Design
Illustrations by Linda Olliver

PRINTING AND PRODUCTION
Catherine Lorrain, Director

NATIONAL SCIENCE TEACHERS ASSOCIATION
David L. Evans, Executive Director
David Beacom, Publisher

1840 Wilson Blvd., Arlington, VA 22201
www.nsta.org/store
For customer service inquiries, please call 800-277-5300.

Lexile® measure: 670L

Library of Congress Cataloging-in-Publication Data
Names: Fries-Gaither, Jessica, 1977- author.
Title: Notable notebooks : scientists and their writings / by Jessica
    Fries-Gaither.
Description: Arlington, VA : National Science Teachers Association, [2016] |
    Audience: Ages 8-11.
Identifiers: LCCN 2016024412 (print) | LCCN 2016025039 (ebook) | ISBN
    9781681403076 (print) | ISBN 9781681403083 (e-book)
Subjects: LCSH: Science--Methodology--Juvenile literature. |
    Notebooks--Juvenile literature. | Scientists--Juvenile literature.
Classification: LCC Q175.2 .F75 2016 (print) | LCC Q175.2 (ebook) | DDC
    509.2/2--dc23
LC record available at *https://lccn.loc.gov/2016024412*

Library edition ISBN: 978-1-68140-379-3

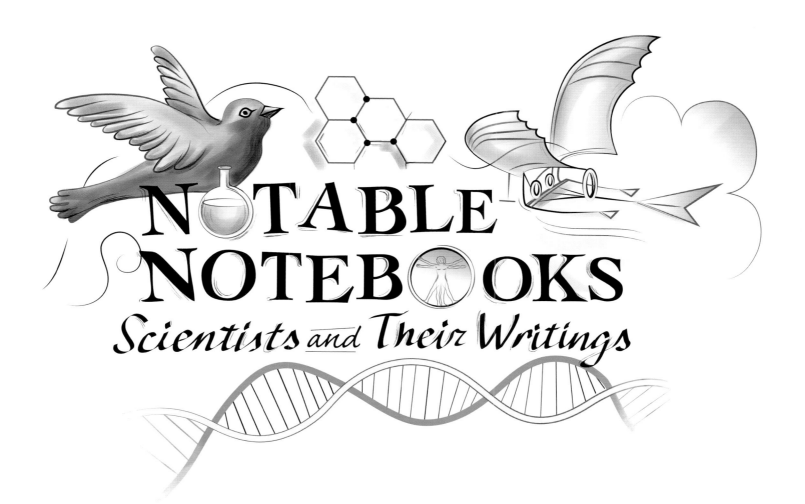

NOTABLE NOTEBOOKS
Scientists and Their Writings

By **Jessica Fries-Gaither**

Illustrated by **Linda Olliver**

NSTA **Kids**
National Science Teachers Association

Arlington, Virginia

SUN → Tree → rabbit → racoon → Fox

Rotate to spin on axis

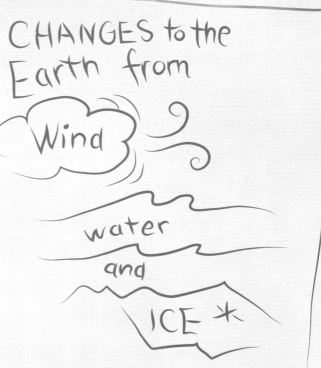

CHANGES to the Earth from Wind water and ICE *

Of all a scientist's tools,
objects rare and common,
the lowly science notebook
is most easily forgotten.

Scientists write in notebooks
about every plant and crater;
notebooks help them understand
what they observe in nature.

What makes a notebook special?
It's a place to think and dream,
to write down thoughts and questions
about all that you have seen.

Weathering Breaks down Rock

Wind

Frozen Water
expands rock and
cracks it

Before   After

Environments

Motion

Oceans

Sea Life

If you find a science notebook,
open it and have a look.
You will surely be amazed
by what's inside this book.

Reading such a notebook
is a great way to explore.
We can learn so many things
from those who came before.

Insects

Animals

Plants

Don't believe me? Then let's go!
Let's travel through time and see
exactly how important
one notebook just might be.

Let's visit Galileo
back in 1641.
He drew inside his notebooks
planets orbiting the Sun.

In his notebook was a model
of thinking that was new.
His ideas, though quite correct,
were not a welcome view.

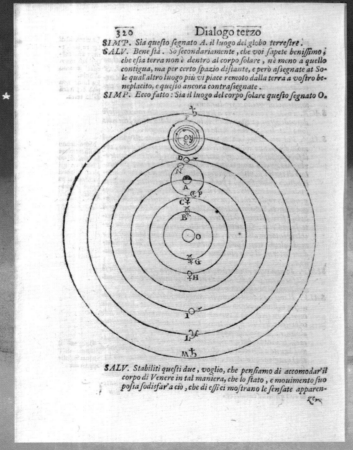

Diagram of planetary orbits by Galileo

Galileo filled up notebooks
viewing the night sky,
observing moons and stars and comets
as they were passing by.

Galileo's evidence
helped imaginations roam.
Other famous scientists
looked at things closer to home.

Isaac Newton was a genius;
he truly did it all.
Complex calculations
in his notebook he did scrawl.

Legend says he thought, "Aha!"
under a shady apple tree.
Whatever's true, he did define
the theory of gravity.

Measurements and data
convey the greatest wonders,
and Sir Isaac Newton's notebooks
contained lots and lots of numbers!

Math's a part of science,
no matter what you do.
But other things, like drawing,
can help you learn it, too.

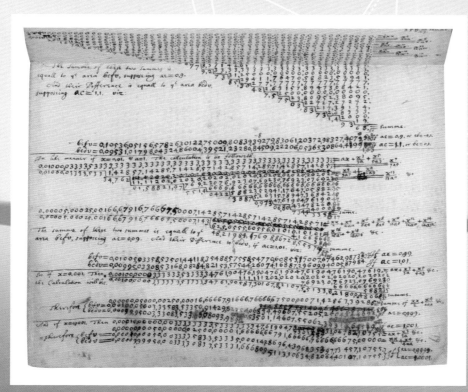

Actual pages in Isaac Newton's notebook

Beatrix Potter was an author.
She loved to write and draw.
But she also was a scientist
who recorded what she saw.

Insects, rocks, and fungi
all graced her notebook pages.
The detail in her drawings is
a treasure for the ages.

Actual page of Beatrix Potter's sketchbook

Ms. Potter used her talents
to answer her own query.
Sketching helped her understand
the fungi's life quite clearly.

Notebooks can be valuable
to organize and review.
They also are essential
when describing something new.

On the rooftop of a bank,
Maria Mitchell could be seen
peering through her telescope
as part of her routine.

On a clear October night
something caught her eye.
Could it be a bright new comet
she saw zooming by?

Indeed, it was as she had thought:
a great discovery!
Miss Mitchell with her careful notes
helped all the world to see.

Notebooks aren't just for notes;
there's more that you can do.
Scientists plan experiments
and then conduct them, too.

Photo of Maria Mitchell in her observatory

Did you know that insects hear?
Surprising, but it's true.
Before Charles Henry Turner,
it was something no one knew.

Dr. Turner studied ants and bees
and all the ways they act.
His experiments uncovered
things we now accept as fact.

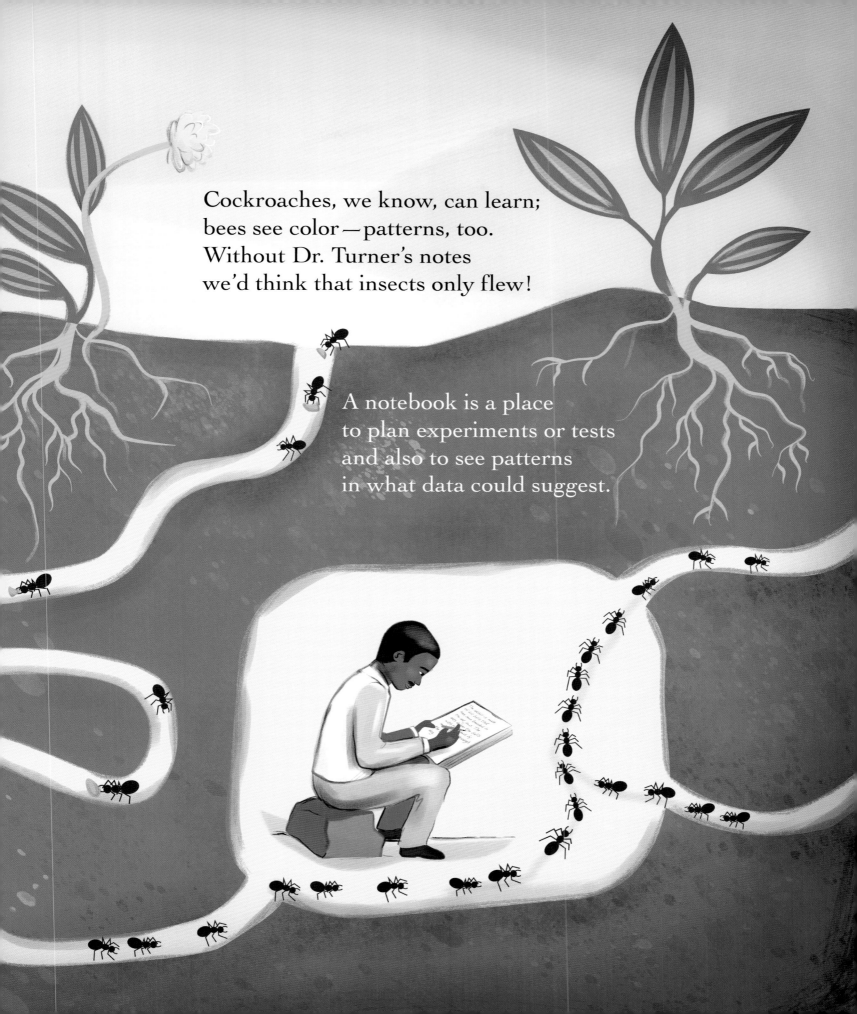

Cockroaches, we know, can learn;
bees see color—patterns, too.
Without Dr. Turner's notes
we'd think that insects only flew!

A notebook is a place
to plan experiments or tests
and also to see patterns
in what data could suggest.

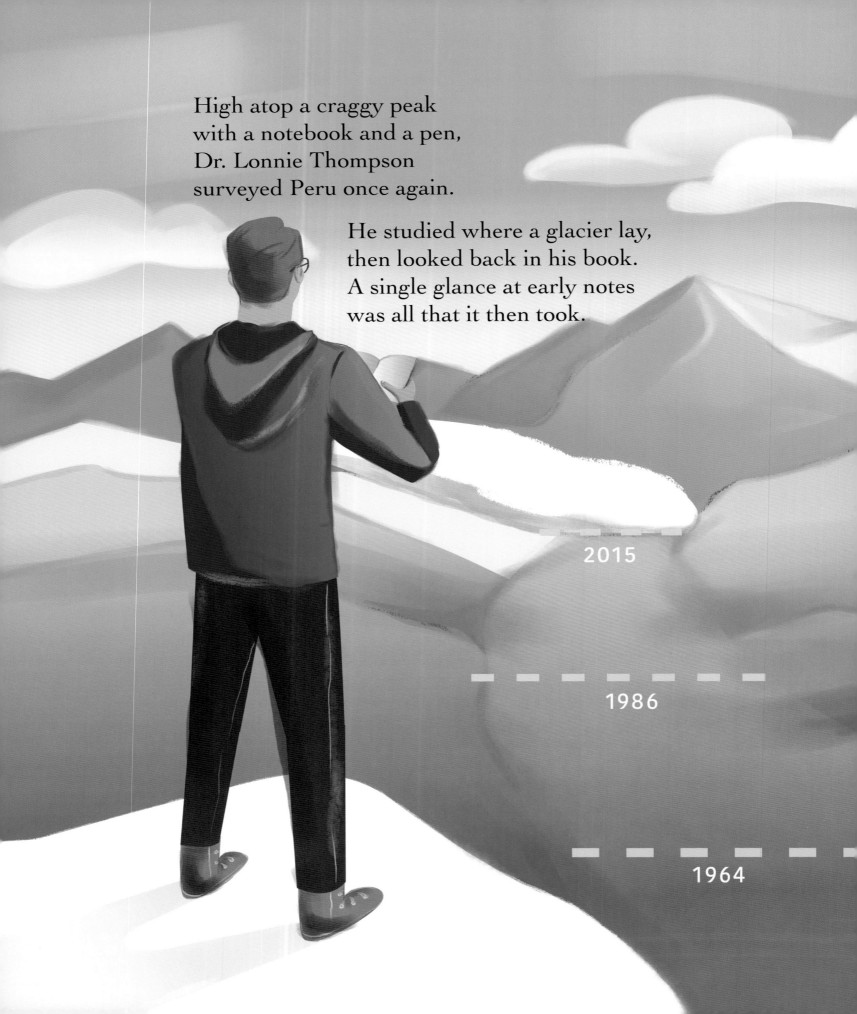

High atop a craggy peak
with a notebook and a pen,
Dr. Lonnie Thompson
surveyed Peru once again.

He studied where a glacier lay,
then looked back in his book.
A single glance at early notes
was all that it then took.

2015

1986

1964

Actual notebook of Dr. Lonnie Thompson

The photos above from Dr. Lonnie Thompson show how much the ice has melted over the years. The top photo was taken in 1978 and the bottom photo in 2004.

"This glacier is retreating;
there's no doubt at all on that.
The world has gotten warmer
since the last time I here sat."

Scientists craft explanations.
They find the missing link.
Good thing that in a notebook
one can reflect and think.

In a forest of Gombe,
Jane Goodall sat quite still.
The chimpanzees were very close,
their nearness such a thrill.

She observed for many years—described their lives and play.
Her notes on their behavior are important still today.

Many a page of journal writing helped her understand
our relatives the chimpanzees and thus her fellow man.

Dr. Goodall took her notes in a remote and wild place.
Our next scientist's notebooks have been to outer space!

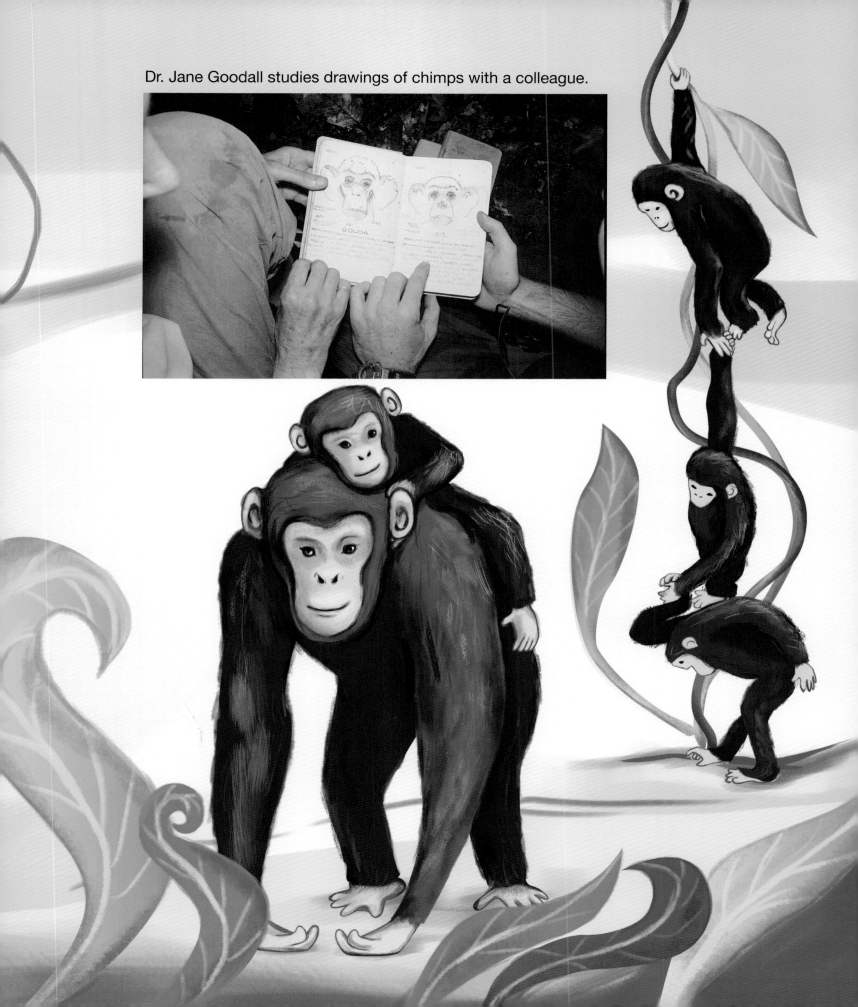

Dr. Jane Goodall studies drawings of chimps with a colleague.

Ellen Ochoa is an astronaut
and a brilliant engineer.
On four short missions out to space,
she explored a vast frontier.

Dr. Ochoa used her notebooks
to describe her NASA missions.
Another set of notebooks
fulfilled other great ambitions.

Ellen Ochoa

Notebooks hold the story
of her various designs.
She used many, many pages
to think, create, refine.

Inventors also use notebooks
to plan, design, and dream.
Sometimes the results they get
are not quite what they seem.

The chemist Stephanie Kwolek —
her job was to invent.
She is now remembered
for a happy accident.

At first, her best discovery
seemed like a big mistake.
Little did she know she'd found
a substance tough to break.

Her notebooks outline all the steps
for inventing this strong strand.
A fiber she called Kevlar
would save lives across the land.

Making sense of data
can be difficult to do.
But if you keep on trying,
then you might find something new.

Kevlar is a super-strong nylon fiber. Because of its strength-to-weight ratio, it can be stronger than steel. Some of the things that Kevlar has made possible include body armor, tires, boats, and airplane wings.

Charles Darwin
NATURALIST
GEOLOGIST

NATURAL SELECTION

THEORY OF EVOLUTION

Charles Darwin wrote in his
while sailing on a boat.
And you'd need to use a mirror
to read what da Vinci wrote!

Marie Curie's findings
helped develop the X-ray.
Did you know her notebook
is radioactive still today?

RADIOACTIVITY

Marie Curie
PHYSICIST AND CHEMIST

PLANT HYBRIDIZATION

Gregor Mendel
BOTANIST

Leonardo da Vinci

MATHEMATICIAN
INVENTOR
ARTIST
ARCHITECT

Their studies may be different,
both in subject and in style,
but the modest science notebook
has been essential all the while.

Gregor Mendel, Albert Einstein,
Rachel Carson, too—
they all relied on their notebooks.
Now, what about you?

Albert Einstein
THEORETICAL PHYSICIST

CONSERVATION

RACHEL CARSON
MARINE BIOLOGIST

You can start your own science notebook! Here's how:

1 Choose a notebook. It doesn't have to be fancy or expensive; even some paper stapled together will do! Your notebook can have lined or unlined paper or even graph paper. Whatever you like best will be fine.

2 Decide what you'd like to study. Maybe you'd like to watch birds or sketch pictures of flowers. Maybe you'd like to try experiments with liquids or look at pond water through a microscope. Whatever you do, your notebook is a great place to record what you are studying.

3 Write about your findings and wonderings. Observing and drawing pictures often aren't enough to understand what you see. Writing about what you find can help you understand it better.

4 Share your work. Just like the work of the scientists in this book, your work is important! Share it with your family, friends, or teachers at school.

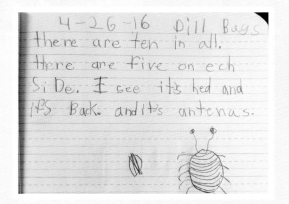

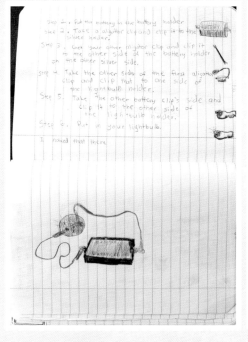

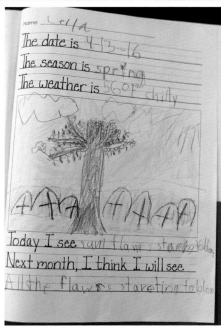

The scientists profiled in this book are a diverse group of men and women who have studied many different branches of science throughout history. Learn a bit more about them here.

Galileo Galilei (1564–1642) lived in Italy. He was a professor of mathematics and also constructed a telescope that allowed him to make detailed observations of objects in space. He discovered several of Jupiter's moons and determined that our Moon's surface is not smooth but is covered by craters and mountains. His observations of Venus provided evidence to support the theory that the Earth revolved around the Sun. This was an unpopular view, and he was accused twice of heresy by the Roman Catholic Church.

Isaac Newton (1642–1727) lived in England. He was a prolific scientist, studying math, astronomy, light, and physics. Newton invented calculus; created a reflecting telescope that he used to study light and optics; and described how objects move, stop, and change direction in his laws of motion. Legend has it that Newton's work on motion and gravity was inspired by an apple falling from a tree. While this cannot be confirmed, his ideas about gravity also helped explain the motion of planets and other celestial bodies.

Beatrix Potter (1866–1943) is best known as the author of children's books such as *The Tale of Peter Rabbit* and *The Tale of Benjamin Bunny*. She was also keenly interested in mycology, or the study of fungi. Her detailed paintings and drawings led her to write a paper describing how fungi reproduce through spores. However, she had to have a male friend present the paper on her behalf at the Linnean Society in 1887 because women were not permitted to attend.

Maria Mitchell (1818–1889) was the first female professional astronomer in the United States. Her father nurtured her interest in astronomy from an early age and taught her to use a telescope. It was on the rooftop of her father's bank that she first observed a new comet, which was known as Miss Mitchell's Comet. Mitchell received a medal for her discovery from the king of Denmark. She went on to become a professor of astronomy at Vassar College.

Charles Henry Turner (1867–1923) was a zoologist and the first African American to receive a PhD from the University of Chicago. Through experimentation, he discovered that insects can hear and can change their behavior based on previous experience. He also showed that bees can see in color and recognize patterns. Turner conducted much of his work without lab assistants or research space. Nevertheless, he invented new techniques for conducting field research and changed our understanding of insect behavior.

Lonnie Thompson (1948–present) studies paleoclimatology, or Earth's past climate, through the analysis of ice cores from mountain glaciers and ice caps in tropical regions. One important project was the study of the Quelccaya Ice Cap in the Andes mountains of Peru. Thompson's work has shown that glaciers around the world are melting, important evidence of global climate change. He and his wife, Ellen Mosley-Thompson, have received recognition and awards for their work.

Jane Goodall (1934–present) spent 45 years studying chimpanzees in Gombe Stream National Park, Tanzania. Through her study of the life and social interactions of the chimps, she was able to challenge two commonly held ideas: Only humans use tools, and chimpanzees are vegetarians. She proved that neither idea is true. Goodall founded the Jane Goodall Institute to support continuing research, as well as a global youth program known as Roots & Shoots. Goodall continues to travel the world as an advocate for conservation and animal welfare.

Ellen Ochoa (1958–present) became the first Hispanic woman in space when she served on a nine-day mission aboard the space shuttle *Discovery* in 1993. She participated in three additional missions, spending almost 1,000 hours in space. Ochoa has degrees in physics and electrical engineering and holds three patents. She is currently the director of the Johnson Space Center.

Stephanie Kwolek (1923–2014) was a chemist who is best known for her discovery of Kevlar, a synthetic fiber stronger than steel. Kwolek discovered Kevlar by accident while conducting research for new fibers to use in tires. Since its discovery in 1964, Kevlar has been used in more than 200 products, including tennis rackets, boats, cables, bulletproof vests, and even cell phones.

Image Credits

p. 8: Public domain. "Dialogo terzo, p. 320 with diagram of planetary orbits, Dialogo di Galileo Galilei, 1632," Portland State University, *http://exhibits.library.pdx.edu/exhibits/show/the-envious-tooth-of-time/item/258*.

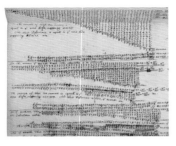

p. 11: Public domain. Cambridge University Library, *http://cudl.lib.cam.ac.uk/collections/newton*.

p. 12: Hygrophorus puniceus by Beatrix Potter. Pencil and watercolour—7 October 1894. Collected at Smailholm Tower, Kelso © The Armitt Trust.

p. 15: Maria Mitchell, Vassar College Digital Library. Public domain.

p. 19: AP Photo/Ricardo Lopez. © The Associated Press.

p. 19: Thompson, Lonnie G. 1978 Qori Kalis Glacier: From the Glacier Photograph Collection. Boulder, Colorado USA: National Snow and Ice Data Center. Digital media.

p. 19: Thompson, Lonnie G. 2004 Qori Kalis Glacier: From the Glacier Photograph Collection. Boulder, Colorado USA: National Snow and Ice Data Center. Digital media.

p. 21: Dave Morgan is showing his drawings of study chimps to Jane Goodall. Michael Nicole/National Geographic Creative.

pp. 28–29: Photos courtesy of Bondi Photography, LLC.